PROGRESSIVE LANGUAGE

GW00708639

a spoken word book
by
Steve Duncan

This book has been purchased with ESF funding for delegates attending the NOMS CFO new futures Cornwall Legacy Conference.

European Union
European Social Fund
Investing in jobs and skills

published by

glennie
communications group

SECOND EDITION, NOVEMBER 2014

Published by Glennie Publishing
a division of Glennie Limited

Copyright © Steve Duncan 2014
Grandma's Philosphy, Mother, Words, The Game,
I am Africa, Hope, Preaching Diversity

Copyright © Steve Duncan and Ian Glennie 2014
Judgement Room, Addiction, Diagnosis of the Youth

All rights reserved.

ISBN

978-0-9927206-0-5

This book is dedicated in its entirety to

My mother,
Geneva Ameretta Duncan

*"Mum ... you taught me better
         than any academic or book ever could"*

Acknowledgements

God. My family, Micheal, Karen and Denise Duncan.
My father, Charles Leopold Duncan!
I am who I am because you loved me.

Lisa Marie Cregan for putting up with me,
sustaining me and helping me stay alive so I can write.

Ian Glennie for helping me to understand
how to be professional and that words are Power.

Marilyn Harrison, my womentor. Thanks for your patience,
compassion and understanding and your continued
belief in me.

Sally Lewis, Suzanne Thompson, Kwesi Ngozi, Micheala
Griffiths and all at New Futures Project. Chantelle Smith for
your continued belief and support. I love you guys!

Sophie Norris for helping with transcription. Mark Harvey for
your photography. Vernon Thorpe for your design.
All freely given.

Preface

Steve Duncan has a gift – the fact that this gift was discovered and nurtured in prison makes it all the more miraculous.

I am deeply privileged to have witnessed Duncan performing his poetry ("reciting" does not do the experience justice) several times now, and as you are reading this book hopefully you have too. If so, you will know that this book doesn't contain Steve Duncan's poetry. Frankly nothing, and certainly not this paperback cover, could contain a force of nature like that.

Yes, these are Duncan's words, but one cannot just read Steven Duncan's true poetry, one experiences it. Duncan's poetry (maybe all great poetry) reaches a different part of the brain -- indeed maybe not the brain at all, maybe the spirit or the flesh. Even reading this book alone in your room, you will find your body moving involuntarily, nodding your head, snapping your fingers, channelling some deeply buried self from generations long past, maybe even trying to spit the words out as quickly, ferociously and melodiously as Steve does on stage.

At the same time, there is something wonderful to have these words on the page – almost as if one can stop time, hit rewind, and play back a Steven Duncan performance in 'super slo mo'.

Do you remember albums? (Forget about vinyl, my kids can barely remember what CDs were for). The thing I miss most about buying albums, besides shopping in actual record stores, was the lyric sheets you got on the inside cover.

Now there was a nerdy quality to these, which I think is why they always made the font so small and illegible. That is, the coolest among us would just listen to the music and get instinctively what it is that a song is conveying. Yet, there will always be a group of us – maybe overly enthusiastic fan-geeks – who need to go that step further and find out precisely what it was that Elvis Costello was mumbling about in the third lyric after the second chorus, or what mysterious meanings were animating Kim Gordon's unintelligible wailing or Flavor Flav's shouts. The quest is to uncover the buried gem, the coded secret that was only available for the true fans.

Like yourself reading this book, I am proud to be counted a true fan of Steven Duncan. I cannot always hear or remember every word he is saying when he is in full-tilt performance, but I know I agree with it instinctually. Thanks Steve, for sharing your gift, and thanks also to fellow fan-geek Ian Glennie for having the insight to see it, to recognise its worth, and to go to such lengths to get it out to the rest of us. That, friends, is poetic justice and long may it thrive.

Shadd Maruna, Ph.D.
Dean and Professor
Rutgers Newark School of Criminal Justice

contents

PROGRESSIVE LANGUAGE

Introduction

This book is made up of a total of over 10,000 words. Not bad as a body of work for a poet.

But what is remarkable is that every word, in its proper sequence, existed first in the memory of Steven Duncan. Because this book is the first time Steve's poems have ever been typed up and reproduced. Before now, these perfectly shaped poems existed only as a quite disorderly collection of hand-written notes in muddled up notebooks as well as, of course, in a beautiful lattice of meaning and sound in Steve's mind.

To hear Steve deliver his poems as a performance artist, without deviation or hesitation, is astounding.

With his black skin and fast-paced delivery, passing listeners might expose their prejudice and take him for a rap artist. But Steve is part of a far more ancient tradition. His words and meaning cut deep.

To hear him perform, the feeling I get is of an old Testament prophet. He is both loving and challenging in his delivery in equal measure.

And don't be fooled into thinking this is a clever trick. I have sat in countless meetings with Steve, where he has summed up in one off-the-cuff laser-sharp sentence or phrase what the rest of us clumsy intellectuals have been discussing and struggling to articulate for half an hour.

Steve first started to take poetry seriously as a vocation when he was in Horfield prison in Bristol. He performed his poem 'Diagnosis of the Youth' (see page 21) to his cell mate from memory.

His cellmate, unsurprisingly, was quite taken aback. He insisted Steve do it again. He then called other cellmates to come and listen. Skip forward six years and Steve now regularly visits prisons to perform to inmates, prison governors and staff. He recently received a standing ovation when still only half way through his poem 'Judgement Room' (page 73).

It is these words, words, words (page33) and also his magical and engaging personality which brings audiences alive.

Steve is part of an ancient tradition of storytellers in rhyme who cut to the heart of the matter.

Steve and I first met when I was interviewing him and recording his poetry for a film for Avon and Somerset Probation Trust.

We hit it off, I think, because we both believe that 'communicating from the heart' is what we were put on this planet to do.

Whereas my 'communication from the heart' tends to the warm and fuzzy, and spreads out diffusely like a summer wind, Steve's communication is direct and vigorous like a big kiss on the cheek or playful punch on the chin.

Steve spent a total of five years in prison or on probation. As he says himself, it was not a deprived or abused background which pushed him into crime. He was lured by the quick money and big ego kick that came from drugs. Although never a violent man, he needed to commit crime to feed his addiction.

For him, 'addiction was stronger than love' as he says in one of his poems (page 43).

Since following the straight and narrow (if being a volcano of creativity and thoughtful elegant poetry could ever be described as narrow) Steve's life has been tough - because of his own remorse, fear and shame as well as the labels slapped on him, in perpetuity, by a judgemental society. But, as Steve sees it, it is also a life blessed by the love and connection with people.

Steve was, I believe, the first unpublished author ever to perform on BBC Radio 4's flagship poetry programme, 'Poetry Please'.

He has won numerous poetry slams, starred at festivals and performed to audiences at theatres, conferences, prisons, universities, schools and clubs - in fact, wherever his most amazing voice and words are willing to be heard.

Steve's biggest regret is that his mother never saw him crime-free and making a living as an award-winning performance poet and justice communicator.

My personal belief and suspicion is that Steve's mother is in heaven looking down with a heart swelled with pride and love.

I'm honoured to call Steve a friend. And every time, every time, I hear or read his words I get the feeling I am sat close to greatness. Not greatness in that puffed-up earthly sense but rather in that deep soul sense of someone who is actively struggling to daily share life and hope with others.

Ian Glennie

Insider Insight

This book of Steve Duncan's performance poetry is one of the products of our collaboration together as 'Insider Insight'. We also work together on training, desistance workshops and arranging events where Steve can perform. Because, as Shadd Maruna points out in his preface, until you have seen Steve perform in person you are only getting half of the experience.

As a society, we claim that we believe in forgiveness and rehabilitation. But the fear we feel for those with a criminal past locks us into prejudices which can block people from living a more positive future. This harms us and others.

Through our work with 'Insider Insight' we hope to challenge those prejudices, ease those fears and set people free.

Ian Glennie & Steve Duncan
Follow us on Twitter: @IanGlennie @BlessheadSteven

Consciously or
subconsciously,
this world
will marry
its memory
of meeting you.

GRANDMA'S PHILOSOPHY

My conscience will never be clear.
See, I will forever hear
the voice of Grandma's philosophy
bellowing at me.
A woman that stood so upright,
her very presence was scary.
This contrasting controversy to popular belief
that age is not really beauty.
See, wisdom was her security.
This voice of visionary
that was constantly killing me softly with profound truth.

She'd echo verbal volleys
that equated to the volume of a whale
and at the same time sing with the subtlety of a starling
on a Sunday morning.
She just kept calling:
"Come kid, come sit."
Eggs, coffee, Weetabix,
prayer and meditation, spiritually fit,
physical food and spiritual food,
this day belongs to you.

And then with the insight of a psychic,
she'd describe everything I'd done wrong last night
and then successfully predict the potential conflict
that was coming in to meet me.
A miraculous feat indeed, but how could it be
because she could barely see?
She was losing her sight but she still had God in her eyes.
Her vision was never compromised.

And she could see through the lies,
and her lips bore the sores
of the sorriest stories of the century,
but she still managed to smile.

Gratitude could never elude her.
She'd mastered the art and arduous task of acceptance.
Been widowed in the Civil War
but she was not a bit bothered
because she knew what we was fighting for.

And she could barely walk, but she swaggered her hips
with the pride of someone that had survived the slave ships
and managed to dance through the storm.
And the wrinkles in her face
were just the slow drawn out pace in the race of perseverance.
And the greys in her hair,
just the glittering of God's grace,
as if she'd been preserved to say something to you.
Another Guru taken for granted.
So now, for Grandma's sake, I stay awake
to a mirage of mistakes I made
when the seed was already planted.

And the only thing I miss more than Grandma
was her philosophy.
Those moments of serenity
where she gently sit me on her knee
and look me in the eye and smile sarcastically and say:
"Kid, it's not about the money, it's about the memories,
the things we leave behind.

Those that breed darkness, and those that feed light,
have got the very power to either mutilate or redefine
the shape of our hearts and shape of our minds."

Memories.
Because that's where legacy lives
and legacy is the greatest gift a human being can give,
because it's only in death that we are fully appreciated.

So kid, keep thinking about the images you want to be giving
for your offspring to live in.
And I don't just mean family, I mean whatever's living.

Consciously or subconsciously,
this world will marry its memory
of meeting you.

Don't look at me,
that was Grandma's philosophy.
See Grandma was deep.
She even said be nice to the trees,
because even the breeze is your companion,
and the sun sees every hand that moves wrongly
and scorches the serenity of its present Karma.

She said if life gets rougher, be calmer.
Because all life is but a sea of drama to be sailed in
and you'd be punished for some of the things you did do
and abused and wrongly accused
for some of the things you didn't.

But just keep forgiving.
Because it's in that forgiveness that you're given
the chance of a life worth living,
otherwise people get to live in your head,
rent free, constantly.
And that's no way to be.

And if we're all so different
why is it that every human being that breathes
leaves his genetic condensation somewhere
within the earth's capacity,
that gathers in the midst
then gets eclipsed
by a vision, that can sometimes look cloudy, and rowdy.
So be careful when you shout
because the universe can hear you.

And the universe will rehearse and reimburse
the language that you adhere to,
pulling you away from the very virtue of good character,
and noble stature,
the emancipation for all decency to match up to.

See, Grandma used to say that at the end of the day,
in judgement's fate,
the only status that really matters,
and grants you any grace,
is embedded in your DNA anyway.
Invisibly encrypted in the skin, festering in the flesh.
Unpeeled to reveal the naked truth
of what harm did you scroll
into the blood and the bones
and where did it flow to?

Or did you find your forgiveness
and make this experience useful and neuter it neutral?

What scars did you carve into the hearts
of those that love you?
What evaporates, departs and resonates as your residue,
and trickles down like constant rain drops of forget-me-nots,
to flood the world of your truth?

See Grandma said we should have bridal ceremonies
for memories that we groom in our hearts
and divorces and funerals for the bad parts.
Because till death does it start.

But this is not really about my Grandma.
This is about me and you and the struggles we go through.
A Grandma that we all need to go to.
A philosophy that we all need to grow through.

And the only thing that I miss more than Grandma
is this philosophy.
This moment of serenity, where I gently use the art of poetry,
to remind you that people ...
this is not about the money, it's about the memories,
the things we leave behind.
Those that breed darkness and those that feed light,
have got the very power to either mutilate or redefine
the shape of our hearts and shape of our minds

Memories,
because that's where legacy lives.
And legacy is the greatest gift a human being can give
because its only in death that we're fully appreciated.

So people ...
keep thinking about the images
you want to be giving
for your offspring to live in,
and I don't just mean family,
I mean whatever's living.

Consciously or subconsciously,
this world will marry its memory,
of meeting you.

She dances
with this
delusion that
babies having
babies
turns kids
into ladies

DIAGNOSIS OF THE YOUTH

Somebody help me diagnose these youth,
because the youth of today
are really mixed up and confused.
You can see in their attitude,
you wonder why they are quick to get violent?
It's just because they are controlled by this fear.
It's the code of the postcodes,
that says you have got to be macho
to get respect from your peers.

So, what, you didn't know?
The social pressure on the male ego to be macho?
Learnt behaviour to a fool
but did it all start at school
where it's progressive common culture
for the kids to be cruel?
Or did they learn it in the home,
where sibling rivalry seems to simulate the tone
and dysfunctional dilemmas get competitively cloned?
We'll evermore explore the whys and the wherefores.

The hierarchy systems debate
constantly, constantly, constantly.
Stop blaming it on rap and hip hop.
It's the parents, it's the family.
It's the media, no, it's TV.
It's the drugs, the alcohol, the social depravity.
It's something in the water maybe.
It's the Terminator movies, no, it's Playstation 3.
They maybe play a small part equally
but the truth is so illusive
that the eye of this generation cannot see.
It's actually a lack of spirituality.

And the hearts and minds have been captured
by yobbish rebellion and thug mentality.

In a world where children should be seen and not heard,
negative attention gives them an identity.
It's like a root that grew into a tree
because the youth are going to go and grow
on what they really see.

They don't want degrees or PHDs or GCSEs.
The only school they want to go to
is the school of reality
cos there's no education like adversity,
no university like the school of hard knocks,
smoking weed and shotting rocks,
drumming your neighbour just to get the latest Nike socks.

Little girls with big breasts
running round in Armani frocks.
Bubbalicious little butts bouncing round the playground
with boastful banter about whose had the biggest.

She don't want Barbie or Cindy.
She wants Gucci, Prada, Fendi,
lipstick and a link so she can tell Wendy,
a fashionable pram with a designer baby.
Could it be? Could it be mentally?

She flirts with this philosophy.
She dances with this delusion
that babies having babies
turns kids into ladies,
maybe.

Maybe, fast track to femininity.
But still it's trial and error till the STD tested,
clap, syphilis, advanced strains of HIV,
and hepatitis thrown into the mix.
But ignorance is bliss.
Ignorance is bliss.

Back in the day of my generation it was all about kiss chase,
Rubik's cube, Action men and Scalextrics.
But nowadays kids want to play with real knives
and real life gun clips.

Because it's no longer the days
when kids used to diffuse disputes with their fists.
See it's never just a straightener anymore,
it's more like a war.
Kids are coming back with 2, 4, 6, 8,
willing to hate.
Sometimes there's even more.
And they're willing to kill
and they're not even sure what for.

What is the cure
for this infectious epidemic that you call murder?
Alternatively, spiritually disaffected.
There's two new board games out there,
haven't you heard?
One's called 'life and its devaluation',
the other 'toy soldiers out to get a reputation'.
They're trying to invest and impress
just to fit in and exist in this identity crisis.
Cultural metamorphosis,
anti-social anarchist,

Rude boys, Afros,
Goths and Emos,
Weirdo types, Yardie hypes,
Gangster wannabes and glamorous gutter snipes,
and the rest in pieces committing suicide.

It's not safe blud, it's not alright.
You're arrogant and rude with no gratitude.
Self piteous fool had it hard done by.
Harping on and honing,
hoarding resentment, ungratefully groaning.
Cos you grew up in the ghetto? No?
You ought to get on a plane and travel to Africa
and watch little kids walk eight miles to get some water.
Living in a shack with no shoes and no food,
walking so far to school
that your feet are bleeding black and blue.
Now that's ghetto.
That's proper ghetto.

Pitiful piknis put things into perspective.
I know it's perplex to correct this
cos everybody's confused about the breakthrough.
There ain't no quick fix route.
What's the point of saluting a solution
which is never going to be plain sailing;
when it's obvious and apparent
that human resources are failing?

Is there a God out there?
I swear to God there better be.
It's going to take a miraculous higher source
to restore them to sanity.

The crux of the calamity
is not, the most misunderstood phrase of modern society,
parental responsibility.

Parental responsibility can also be deemed as the ability
to recognise that you did your level best
to raise them properly
but didn't succeed.

Let go with love, let it be.
Not resentful, remorseful, angry or guilty.
It's their journey, their culture, their destiny.
What do you want to be - a parent or a control freak?

Parental responsibility cannot be guaranteed.
It's dependent upon their ability
to respond to your ability to parent successfully.
And right now kids, the ghetto needs some heroes,
so the onus is on you to go find a new reality.
Be brave enough to be the change that you want to see.

Go forth in grace and gallantly embrace
your ambition with passion.
Revolutionise the stigma.
Empower the enigma.
Be the first to recognise and realise
that the first step to recreating your world
is to recreate your culture.

And last but not least,
this fashion legacy you want to leave for my grandbabies ...
"Pull your jeans up ... please!"

I have a
dream,
a vision for
the mind,
a new pair
of glasses
restoring
eyesight.

PREACHING DIVERSITY

I love you,
I love you and you and you and you
and every culture through and through,
I just intuitively do.

Those endless evaluations to expose equality for me
are somewhat needless to go through.

I'm non-partial to that social prejudicial farce
that would have me making judgements
round the outskirts of your mast and past.
Race, colour, creed, breed, sexuality.
I'm miffed and mystified by that twisted mentality.

I'm so tired I can't be assed to analyse
the who, the what, the how, the when,
the whys and wherefores,
or who's really who.

I'm so deep.
I've completely outgrown and surpassed
any kind of history that will keep me trapped
in negative views where my history's been cruel.
For real blud.

Acceptance being a fight
but, in spite, with every breath that I breathe
just increases the belief that I'm right.

From I look into your eyes,
beneath the glare and the fear
my mentality will rise to recognise
you're just a human.

We're just human beings,
trying to find the balance between doing and being,
learning and seeing, fighting and fleeing.

I begin to get a sense of that
immense, intense,
intimate, intriguing,
intricate, intrinsic-ate,
ineffable, immeasurable,
immortal, internal oneness.

That wholesome, that spiritual vibe,
the interconnectedness to the very virtue
of a joyous miraculous mystic
that we call life.

Why, you look so surprised?
What ... you don't believe a big black man with gold teeth?
But who are you to question my social integrity?

Shed blood bleed for my twisted seed.
Shed blood bleed for my twisted seed.
Leave me alone BNP, no please.

Because I have a dream,
a vision for the mind,
a new pair of glasses restoring eye sight.

Because I recite uplifting rhymes
for minds that are blind
and I spy with my little eye
that natural mystic in the sky
beginning with L-O-V-E.

Bringing your mind
into the cultural exchange of humanity,
a one stop shop,
because I could be you,
and you could be me.

That place we can only purchase
with proper moral currency,
utopia for free,
equality, diversity,
emancipation from a distinct entity,
freedom from cultural captivity,
opportunity, liberty,
redemption, harmony,
unity, peace, integration, democracy,
social justice, freedom of speech.

I'm a preacher.
I'm preaching diversity.
I'm sorry if it's soppy.
I'm sloppily slapping solidarity on spiritual treason
because the quest to see and treat someone as human
doesn't need any reason.

Those hurry come up hypes and stereotypes,
portrayed for the eyes of society's vision.

Well tell television to tell my vision.
No you're not a racist, because you listen to Marley.
But deep down you really believe
that all I'm good for is promiscuity,
selling weed and succeeding in the entertainment industry.

With white people,
it's you're responsible for slavery,
and you can't dance,
and all you ever eat is fish, chips and mushy peas.
But yes we'll have the women ... please, please, please.

With Asians,
it's the association with smelly breath,
the invasion of shops and take-aways.
But still complete admiration on a Saturday night
when you're pissed up eating curry, naan and raisins.

With Arabs and Muslims
it's female degradation,
acts of terrorist salvation.

Everybody's guilty.
We fluctuate from love to hate,
with selective memory we cultivate
convenient appreciation for different racial contribution
considering those common manifestations.

Let's stop being so serious and take the piss out of creation.

I'm a preacher.
And my God's got a sense of humour.

Envision with me
how cool would it be
to wake up in the morning
and see every police officer in this country
armed with a japatti,
sprouting dreadlocks, speaking fluent Swahili?

Because one day
elderly white women
are going to look out their window
and see hardcore yardies sowing their seeds,
planting their weeds instead of smoking them,
baby-sitting their grandbabies
whilst they tango down to Tesco.

And I hope and I pray that one day,
elderly black women will be chauffeur driven
by Ronnie and Reggie Kray,
depicting scenes of that classic epic,
albeit the opposite,
'Driving Miss Daisy.'

Maybe then you will see,
maybe then we'll see,
the beauty of diversity.

I love you,
I love you and you and you
and definitely you,
I just intuitively do.

Thank you.

These
words have
stripped me
of absolutely
everything
and left me
with nothing
but just my
vulnerability

WORDS

As it was written in the beginning,
there was nothing.
Nothing but one power, one force,
this source that stood in the realm of neutrality,
this energy of creative aspiration.

Some call it God,
but without religious conviction
or spiritual description
let's keep it simple.

See from this vocal realisation,
It fuelled a formulation of planes and plantations
that spoke life into rotation.
This power of communication
that moulds the manifestation of beings to be human,
like you and me.

So in actuality,
words speak louder than actions
as fractions of our persona.
Because my words are constantly transcending me
They're the past that I run from
and the future that I hope to be.

Because all words are just a journey,
the first utterance of reality.
Because whether based in truth or based in deceit,
I will catch up to what I speak.

Words,
Words,
Words.

So before you ask me what my name is,
what my game is,
am I trying to be famous?
I say, people ...
In and of itself,
that's just shallow and aimless.

I ain't got time to try to be the greatest,
my motivation's based in spiritual status,
so these words mean so much more to me.

I want every poet, from every generation,
to attach my name to the innermost quotations of inspiration.
I want to be written into biblical ballads of psalms
and get praises from the angels.
I want to make God happy that he invented language
because Lord I get bored with these conventional standards.
And I know that there's no feat
that will defeat me quicker
than trying to be Jesus.
But I would like to be the cross
in-between Shakespeare and Jay-Z with a Gospel chorus.

I want these words to be absorbed in all four corners.
I want these words to speak to trees
and get sucked in by the phorrus.
I want nature to nurture this voice
as a resounding chorus
gospel of the heart
without the aid of a dictionary
or thesaurus.

God given, natural intuition,
wisdom of words that defied definition.
I am driven by articulate ambition.
I want to penetrate planes so deep
that they reverberate around the surface of Uranus.
And that's Uranus and not your anus.

There's no deviation in the presentation
of this all-oral orchestration.
My linguistics don't ass lick for no affirmation.
Yeah, damn right I'm trying it.

Because if you ain't buying it, I'm going intergalactic.
I'm pushing this stuff out to the aliens
if you earthlings ain't responding.
Because these words are too good to be wasted.

And I pause, as if I've forgotten my words,
as I listen to the ghosts of my vocabulary
whispering back at me:
"Steve, be realistic"

Ok, Ok, Ok
I guess what I'm trying to say is,
I just don't want these words to be dismissed.
I want them to be seductive and possessive,
constructively caressing your senses,
painting pictures of letters that kiss
this artful adaptation of affluent behaviour
with animations that are non-aggressive, non-violent,
non-derogatory, non-misogynistic.
No nigger, no bitch, no verbalistic bull shit.

Because my words are reflective,
connected to the change that I want to see.
Cos these words are words that I want to be.
Exclusive, conducive
to the uplifting of your consciousness.

I want to hold, mould and captivate
the human heart and human mind.
Be the Holy Grail,
the brail to the blind.

This narrative has negated any need
to be offensive or rude.
I got the spiritual food.
See these words can be eaten.
They can literally be tasted.
Lucid lyrics that surpass your lips
and get digested in your spirit.

I want to wrap these words around you
like a winter blanket,
turn your coldness into calmness,
harnessed in the heat of the friction
of the lyrics that are rhythmic.
The intrinsic infusion of muse into spoken verse
that your feelings can dance with.

Chance is they won't make as much money
as my drug selling counterparts
and they may not obtain fame, critical acclaim, accolade,
Hip Hop prestige or awards at glitzy ceremonies.
Maybe they'll just hang in the balance of humility
or echo the soliloquy of my own thinking.

Cos I'm never sleeping,
keeping eyes wide open without blinking
constantly looking for
words, words, words
of love, love, love.

Cos if love don't love these words
then nothing else could ever be enough.
And if you don't love me,
trust me, poetry does.

She told me and tells me every night.
She said if I left her side, she could never survive.
She said if I withdrew these words
she would commit suicide.

And I'm not saying that poetry needs me.
I'm saying that these words believe in me
and are never leaving me.
They are irretrievably breaking down boundaries,
literally giving the illiterates back some literacy.

Playing crosswords and unpuzzling the cryptic,
spelling corrections for dyslexics,
sequencing words of significance,
writing reference for reverence.

Opening your mind and giving you the clues
and the rest is up to you.
This is grammar that generates its own genre.
The generation with a new view.

I found a crayon that colours in figures
and scribbles scripts
to make kids act better.

Because these words are like a jigsaw,
there's a puzzle in every letter,
and I'm out here playing scrabble
trying to re-piece the broken bridges of ignorance
so we can step across together.

I'm never letting letters go from this flow.
I'm hanging on for dear life,
like they was all that I owned.

See these words have to fetch more than scores of ten.
The only slams they are slamming into
is the hearts of men.
The only competition
is the rigorous rendition of repetition
to reinvent the descent of a poet
that repents with his pen.

So let's not let this be a vision of profanity or vanity.
Just touch the souls of those
who feel like they've got nothing left
when it comes to faith in humanity.

And I'm not asking you to have any faith in me,
but please, please, please,
find your words to have faith in when you speak.
The language that motivates your own self belief,
words that can retrieve and bring relief to your spirit
when it's deflated and deceased.

Cos I don't want these words to die
and wither by the wayside.
I want them to win the Noble Peace Prize.
I wish them ever-lasting life.

I want them to reside in pride
and be the cash in the pockets of panache,
the suit and tie, the elegance,
that eloquence of contemporary relevance,
that withstanding of all trial,
to be the proof and evidence
that you can,
actually,
absolutely,
speak your life better.

I want these words to frazzle the brain waves
of my Frenemies.
You know Frenemies ...
those people that smile in your face
but behind your back
they use words and imagery
to slyly defile your personality
and insult your integrity.

I want to show all the haters and doubters
that live in my past,
that this artist has mastered the art of his craft,
and now these words are fighting,
defending everything
that the benefit of this speech
can possibly be.
Cos my words are like weaponry to me.

And I wear my words on my sleeve
as proud as can be.
It's the equivalent of golden artillery to me.

I relish it, cherish it,
polish and embellish it,
on a daily basis.

Spitting missiles into the misguided minds
of those that don't define themselves
through rhyme and reason.

I sense sentences that see solace for all seasons.
Words that weather the storm of the abnormal
because poetry is too deep to be formal.

But of course there are those
that don't understand
the science of poetry,
the therapeutic value
that this holds for me,
for us, we poets.

I am prone to prose and philosophy
that parries the negative
and phraseology that promotes the positive.
Because these words ...
these words, these words, these words
they may be misremembered in the archives of history,
but wherever they go,
they will always, always exist
in the intimacy of my energy.

Because this is all I have
and all I see,
all I want to do
and all I want to be.

Because these words have stripped me
of absolutely everything
and left me with nothing
but just my vulnerability.

And now I've got constant verbal diarrhoea
I just keep spitting, dribbling,
trying to catch these words.
They keep slipping and sliding,
and I won't stop till they make more noise
than heaven and hell colliding.

Because I can't stop, won't stop
till we all wake up to the realization
that what we say is just as valid as what we do.

So whatever you do,
remember ...
words, words, words,
your words,
your words
are watching you.

I'm Addiction,
and when
I'm active I'm
stronger than
love

ADDICTION

I've mesmerised and mystified
the mystics of the ancient wise
and I've baffled the greatest doctorates and scientific minds
of our synchronised time.
Because I exist in the spirit of the greatest conspiracy.
They call me Addiction.

I am the disease.
I am the I am of all I ams.
I'm the triumphant ego building scam.
I'm the insidious illusion colluding to confuse your plans.
I'm the kamikaze kidnapping of the mind
and the whole of the attention span.
I'm the preoccupation ransom payment plan.

I've captivated feelings but I'm promising freedom,
release and relief in ease and comfort, peace of mind.
But paradoxically I'm a compulsive impulse
to indulge in seductive suicide.

I'm that two-faced devil-playing serpent's grace.
The apparently choice-less voice of fate.
I'm the delightful sight of Eve's apple.
I'm that first high, the deceptive lie,
the justification, the excuse, the alibi.
The rationalisation and gratification of temptation,
arousing the angst anxious appetite for destruction.

I'm that sinister sinfulness
that swerves amidst the glitz and the glamour.
I'm that cocky tipsy smarmy swagger.

I'll exalt you to the stars
and watch you flutter to the gutter,
encaptured in that wrath of rapture
rolling reefers to revert you to the grim reaper.

I'm pleased when you're six feet beneath
receiving wreaths and I've blessed you with diseases.

I am the degradation, the desolation,
the destroyer of species,
them legions of leaches,
the suckers that succumb to blood sucking scum,
those intravenous veinless creatures.

The obsessive obese beast,
the gluttonous over-eating feast of fury.
The overdose obnoxious gross negligent
prone home to the luck lustrous infrastructure
of self-centred pleasure.

The me, myself and I,
self-will run riot that kills animal instinct.
Seven deadly sin thrilling fatal fairground attraction.

I'm that roller-coaster ride that's never satisfied.
I'm the dodgem of death, the waltzer of woes,
the carousel of cravings.

I'm the candy-floss that moulds and metamorphoses
into different flavours, tastes,
then shapes the behaviour.

I make manifest in food and sex
and cybernet connects,
repetitive texts,
gambling, shopping
and credit card debts,
et cetera, et cetera, et cetera.

I'm that twist in the very fabric of nature
extracting the worst aspects of your character.

I'm that spiritual death,
the targeted, defective hit,
the emotional eclipse.

The prickle in the prick of a pin
shooting at the speed of light
laughing at the harm reduction rate
of hero to heroine and prostitute to pimp.

I'm the grouch, the gouch,
the chained and untamed.
And you know I'm the nose
that nobody knows
better than cocaine.

Nonsensical, false-pretence
alcoholic bum and bench mentality.

I'm the crack in the reflection of perceptive reality.
The mirror image mirage of cosmetic insanity.
I'm the ugliest form of vanity,
the most profound profanity.

This curious calamity,
the debacle of debauchery,
debonair delusion of a distorted personality.

I'm non-partial, prejudicial to scale or class,
surpassing the vastness of intellect, culture, creed or race.
Debasing the face value of shame.
I savagely shift the equilibrium of relationships,
and with all things being equal,
emotional appeal won't seal my prevention.

I'm sibling separation, maternal manipulation,
the evil revelation in all relations.

I'm the devil's advocation
of the never-ending end
of all things bright and beautiful.
I'm beyond the bond and above the above.

Because I'm Addiction,
and when I'm active,
I'm stronger than love.

See I'm taller than tall
and all I call, one and all,
will fall before me.

Because hell have no fury on humanity like I.
Because I am fly,
the fly-through thief in the night,
that soars higher than hindsight.

But I'll never get into heaven.
So I'm hovering somewhere
between defence and consequence.

I'm sitting on a fence of moral resolution,
a slithering conniving sliding snake,
spitting venom at the solution.

I'm that slippery slope,
the hazardous hole,
waiting for you to fall
so I can take control.

I mix and I blend, cocktail carousing.
Patiently waiting for the party.
Send invitations under the guise of the befriended.

From time beyond, until time extended,
until the intervention of God's revenge
I will exist as a gift in the present.
So stay awake to my presence.

Because I am
the Phenomenon,
the Beast
of Addiction.

Just give
me back the
power of
opportunity,
the choice to
be the source
that salvages
my own
salvation

I AM AFRICA

I – am – Africa.
Because ego aside,
I'm the centre of this universe and steadfast in gravity.
Because no matter which way the wind flows and I flee,
I'll never be free of the heritage that is imparted to me.
Because Africa is me.

Inherently, genetically,
the rhythmic blood line that flows from a heart beat
that hollows and echoes
at the slow mode of a slave's feet.

And I'm trudging that triumphant trod of destiny,
needing rest for the weary.
I'm weak at the knees.
Because I'm so tired, I got bags under my eyes
in which I carry my pride
and the tears that I cry
ripple into the river of denial.

I'm calypso cracked out to the max
with a broken back
trying to resist this soul sickness that's been inflicted
and no voodoo, no witch doctor can fix it.

I'm suffering from the dialysis of a diasporas separation,
the drinking of a diluted dialect,
accumulation of cultural constipation,
volcanic verbal diarrhoea,
the anguishful archaeological amnesia.

The indigestion of an ideology that salutes freedom
when the irony is
my identity and independence
is infamously still in its infancy
and it basically renders me an alien
in my own space.

My chronological status can be equated to the fact
that I don't even know my own age.
Because, literally, literacy was a hand-me-down
of the last half century
and I didn't have any education to be able to calculate.

Confused Yoruba youth,
singing Ashanti psalms to Gods that ain't listening.
I'm praising origin over religion
because I've been pimped and I've been raped
and I've been downtrodden, and I've been blamed,
but I still got faith which sits on the horizon.

See my diligence ain't fading,
I'm parading the brazen black skin of ebony
and the white 'kin teeth smile of ivory
and I'm tough like the elephant's tusks.

I'm the roots, the resurrection,
the ghosts, the soul, the fifth generation
of Salasie, Mandingo, Kunta Kinte, Biko.

My spirit's pining, mining
for that one in a million diamond,
searching for the content of a character that's golden.
And my native tongue's been stolen.

But the only reason I'm speechless
is because words defy my beauty.
So there's so much more to me than just my history
and missing my mystery.

My bosom is the blossoming of a bold and fertile seed,
but the broken borderless boundaries
of embezzlement and greed
will always destroy me.

The internal corruption, the conflict, the controversy
which tears me apart as an entity
and renders me a split personality.

Because one side of me is dying
and yet the other side of me is full
of music, dance and philanthropy.

See my mind is starving
yet my belly is full of a fruitful economy.

I'm blessed with the jiggy jiggy jungle hips
and the bojangle bongo jeans,
but the dance of freedom is still eluding me.

Stuck in limbo between watered down soulful streams
of my own flow,
and deserted desert drought planes,
drifting.
A spiritual being in a human existence,
listening to musical misfits spit shit
in the expansion of gangster languages.

Because I'm a natural Negro
but somehow now, my ears have been exposed
to the reverbatory tribal frequency
which translates into nigger, nigger, nigger,
and the echoes of history
have no encore for this vocabulary.

See we've lost our mentality
and found MTV, television,
the drug of the nation.
The radioactive infiltration of an industry's enslavement.

Because niggers don't exist in the spirit of Africa
and I will die before I become one
for your entertainment.
Because this is not about applause from the audience.
This is about the ordinance of freedom.

I'm not an activist, I'm an alarmist.
I'm not a revolutionary, I'm a realist.

See, this is not some preachy speech to arouse reparation.
Because evolution will unravel and demystify
the mystic myth of separation.

Because apartheid means
there ain't a part you can hide from God's hand,
sewing and sealing the seed of one soil,
that stems from one plantation
and develops into one nation
and grows in revelation.

A higher state of consciousness
that connects the dots of symbolic faces
and simultaneously graces
one source of one trace to one race in all places.
And that can't be equated in your atlases.

This is the geography of spirit.
This is the longitude of lessons that needed to be learned.
The latitude of attitudes that needed to be turned,
inwardly.

The biggest bigotry comes from my own hypocrisy
and the fact that I've watched my own people suffer
and did not do a damn thing
and that's the atrocity.

Which results in the disurbanisation of my own persona,
the colonisation of my own Karma,
the abolition of responsibility.

Because the only thing necessary for failure to succeed
is for everybody to need to believe
it's everybody else's responsibility.

See, we need to safari on a journey
of our own self discovery,
a wake up to the ugliness that we seldom notice.

The shame in the observation of a game
that we called wildlife.
The hunter over the hunted.
The powerful over the lame.

Because the way us humans treat each other,
brothers and sisters,
makes those animals look tame.

So, don't lip service me silent sighs of sympathy
or advocate for active aid for which I'll seldom ever get
but yet still perpetuates a ripple effect
which just propels me into more debt.

Just give me back the power of opportunity,
opportunity to constructively reconstruct
my own resources,
the choice to be the source
that salvages my own salvation.

So from the quagmire of the fragile existence
I will persist to be the greatest success story
of the twenty-first century
and that's not prophecy,
that's destiny.

So you can choose to use your energy
and come and invest in me
own a lease in this legacy
or kick back in anticipation
and watch me be the transformation
of mud huts into mansions,
and shanty towns into success,
and death and sickness into evolution
in the knowing I'm God blessed.

Because I – am – Africa.
I'm that Zulu spear
piercing through the periphery of propaganda.

I put the Amen into the Amin
that was the harming of Uganda.

I'm that first voice, the last hand,
intricately woven from the wisdom of the womb,
this belly of the motherland,
Africa.

And I choose to use poetry,
as a proverbial vision of victory,
that onerous exoneration from a war
that involves no nuclear,
just the unfolding of a faith that's focused and clear.

See, I can hear the uprising coming.
My tongue can taste the freedom in the air.
But, my greatest beauty,
that arises out of the surprising fact
that I've never actually been there.

But who really cares?
Just as long as I understand,
that I – was – Africa
before I became this man.

A myriad of
moons could
never move
or minimise
your mystery
to me

MOTHER

Because she was a woman
who wondered in wisdom
without wasting a single wish
on anything negative.

Talked of a life based on truth,
living testimony,
the sum totality
of everything this world should ever be.

Princess of peace,
passionately pedantic with spiritual principles.
Mixed the melanin in my skin.
Fascinating fallopian tube
which bore fruit to produce
a rebellious youth like me.

And how I took that miracle of life for granted.
Because women are so unique;
that sacrificial painful process, enforced responsibility.

The burden of walking around for nine months
with a bump in the belly
when daddy had so much fun sewing that seed.

The umbilical uprising which unifies and defines
the equity of everything she hoped I would be.

The illustrious energy,
the indelible intensity
that inspires integrity
incessantly, immeasurably
held emotionally.

Obsessively blessed with another three
in which she distributed love perfectly.

Afro-Jamaican cocoa butter queen,
visionary with a dream,
female heroine, Negro Shero.

The cultural captivation of feminine admiration.
The excellence of sexual visual elegance,
epitome of etiquette, absolute of blackness,
deeper than a river that could flow through the abyss.

More beautiful than a butterfly that flirts with the sky
and then stole the suspense on a sweet summer's night.

The heavens used to sing for Mama.

If the clouds could converse,
they'd convey and confirm that my mum
was the original Cleopatra.

She put the growl into Grace Jones.
The most boombastic butt of the blacksploitation error,
that effortless flirtatious endeavour,
sexily dancing with desiderata,
moving amongst the haste placidly.
Reminiscent of a fairytale story,
persona so neat,
her voice was so sweet.

Bed time stories were soothing, healing, easing,
appeasingly pleasing, appealing;

Like the sound of piano keys getting played
by a ghetto-personified Elton John
at six o'clock in the morning
when you're just not sleeping.

Are you feeling my reasoning?
The nostalgic nature of nurturing nappies
getting changed in exchange for playing games
with my smelly ass.

I wasn't washed,
I was baptised in a bath.
Spiritually cleansed
and Mummy used to laugh
every time I used to fart.

Breast milk on tap for this spoilt brat,
so particular and picky.
Mum I'll attribute blame to you,
it's your damn fault I enjoy sucking.

The devil's trying to get us,
so execution of that lust
was a childbearing must.

We were spiritually spoon-fed Sunday school
in small doses Mama said
for the forces that oppose us.

On the whole I was raised in a household
where love could be defined as organic, orgasmic,
overflowing compassionate control.
No crescendos.

Domestic disputes were dissolved on a down low
so as not to raise babies that were crazy.

The only time I ever really remember mum getting angry
is when she was struggling in the kitchen.
Juggling, multi-tasking, jerking up chicken.
Samurai chopping vegetables and kung-fu kicking
the butts of little kids
that wasn't doing the washing up,
up rise to discipline.

Mama's kitchen was a saving grace, sacred space,
thoroughly inspected, ninja protected.
In my abode, there wasn't any bellies rumbling.

We were seriously seduced with stupendous stews
and dapper dumplings,
proper plaintains,
yummy yams and boomy bammys.
Set adrift upon a memory bliss
of bubbalicious banana fritters,
the intensive incentive for homework presented
on time.

Spare the rod and bless that child, the supple self-sacrifice.
The only woman that ever waltzed out of my life,
given everything,
unconditionally requesting nothing in return
and yet still seems satisfied.

In hindsight, I wish I had the foresight
to forecast the futility of fate
that would feeble her frame and fade her away.

Not in vain, never faithless.
Strong in spirit, stricken in flesh.
Attested with the diagnosis of cancer in the breast.

I couldn't appreciate the implications of the affliction,
the severity of her condition.
In that ritual of dependency
I just became accustomed to the assumption
that mum would live forever
just like all kids do.

She loved God so much she was bound to pull through.

On the twenty-sixth of December nineteen ninety two,
this vicious vexation came and reversed
the virtue of my vicissitude.

Singing verses of disillusionment,
cursing, rehearsing, visions of hearses,
howling at the moon, screaming,
asking God to help me see
beneath the smothering darkness
and over the opaque reality that actually,
angels don't always overcome adversity.

So don't you kill my fantasy.
Don't tell me Mummy weren't an angel.
At least have the decency to convince me
that there must have been an angel within,
otherwise you steal my hope,
and you steal my dream
and I punch you on the chin.

What, you see this as sentimental sarcasm
because you can't unravel or unfathom
more of the deepness at which my soul bleeds?

At funerals, flirtatious slip service
that fuels the feud of foolish phrases
like "Son, don't cry and everything will be alright".

But how the hell am I supposed to not cry
as a kid who'd had his mum kidnapped
and been deprived of the angelic plight I cry?

I cry, I cry, I cry.
I'm way too stuck in that solace of selfishness
to live and let die.
I'm substituting with substances to get high.
I'm riding the emotional roller coaster.

I'm gallivanting and garnishing that guilt trip.
I'm swimming in shame
for everything I am, was, and never could be,
the unfound, the unknown, the unseen.

Mum, can you forgive me?
For all those nights when I stole your emotional security?
That torment of uncertainty,
the audacity, temerity,
the torturous tossing and turning, tumbling,
systematically playing drums of tantrums in your head.

Must have been the metaphorical equivalent
of the anguishful anticipation
of hovering over a Semtex bomb strapped beneath your bed.

Addiction, robbery, burglary, truancy,
disappearing acts.
Hence being terrified of telephone correspondence
in which death would have blessed
the suspense with no recompense.
But I sense that in your infinite wisdom of wealth,
I know that you know that I needed help.

Just a little boy with an over-inflated ego,
struggling to develop a deeper sense of self
that went to hell to get some help.

I'd never choose to excuse this abuse.
I'm under no false pretence,
that Mummy would defend my right
to amend an attempt to be all things to all men.

Because all is well that ends well
in the quest that's never ending
and Mum, I've made my mistakes but I've changed now
I'm clean, I'm God-seeking
and at least I've stopped offending.

But guess what Mum,
perfection is still pending.

And I don't know if you can hear me, see me or feel me,
but I'm still struggling, still searching,
for want of a better word of wisdom
that would never wither,
but forever deliver the justification to your legacy.

Because Mother, Mother, Mother,
wherever you are:
You are the star in my trek,
the guiding force, the Jedi night,
a billion light years of my delight.
A million and one suns could never undo
what this son means to you.
A myriad of moons could never move or minimise
your mystery to me.

Because you are, and always will be,
the very existence of a persistence to pursue bliss.

Because Mother, Mother, Mother,
there isn't enough dialogue in the dictionary,
there ain't enough lyrics in the language,
there isn't any prose or any poems,
that could ever bring my love for you
to a finish.

Our hierarchy that keeps the rich upraised and the deprived depraved

THE GAME

Most of us live life on such a superficial plane.

See this is all just a game,
and it's a shame we don't see things the same,
and the blame seems to fall in the wrong spaces
because life ain't fair.

It's just one big oasis
of different castes, classes and races
and ignorant faces,
gods and money and hierarchy statuses,
lords and masters searching for greener pastures,
well advanced in a stance of their own selfishness,
well adjusted to the injustices,
writing laws and getting applause
for a cause that they're not really concerned about,
whilst showering us with sanctimonious vows
that drench our doubt
and facilitate a false sense of security.

We're constantly concentrating
on this ballot box paradox,
puppets talking, sucking us in,
culturally nurturing the needy into falsely believing
in this external quest for happiness,
this sense of contentedness,
the wanting to come home.

The longing to be complete,
forever searching for the stars
whilst never fully living
in the world beneath our feet,
the one that we call reality.

The one that screams at us to absorb its normality,
the one that shouts at us to wake up
to the criticality of our time,
to think critically,
to reason our being and question our minds,
to re-examine the dissatisfaction of our actions,
the removal of what it means to be human.

Although we try to fight and deny,
at some point in time,
all minds must inquire
and desire insight
into the meaning of life,
that "who feels it knows it" present moment,
intuitive, intelligent
thoughtful contemplation.

The "why is life happening to me?"
The "how and what kind of person do I want to be?"
The "Is this all there is? Is this the plight of our fallacy?"

An analysis of the biggest:
"If God really exists, then why would he permit
so much suffering and tragedy
and yet live at ease with what it sees?"

Or drift off into the
"As long as it's not happening to me" syndrome
and everything's jiggy.
We're ultimately humanoids, devoid of sensitivity,
married to this mirage of moral complacency.

It's as if we just drift in existence
in this bubble of presumed neutrality,
because if the suffering of this world becomes a distinct entity
that's a form of insanity.

When the ignorance of deaf ears can only hear
the footsteps to their own journey,
and the blood of our hearts can only beat in connection
with the force of its own anatomy:
"Why are we so attuned to this frequency of dis-harmony?"

We need look no further than the luxury of our TV screens.
Because news reels tonight probably won't contain footage
of the progress of lunar flight
or even the advancement in cure for AIDs or cancer.
But, by all probability, you can guarantee
there will be terrorism, war, rivalry, ravagery
and child to child savagery.
The latest statistics on crime, addiction,
unemployment and poverty.

And whilst we wine and dine tonight
and absorb those flavours,
and savour those tastes,
will we save some grace,
for that kiddy on the other side of the earth's face
that is pining and dying for the waste?

As we desensitise our deeds to the needs of the needy,
and re-feed on the vomit of our hierarchy
that moulds this monopoly,
that keeps the rich upraised and the deprived depraved,
and the rest are just suckers and pawns getting played.

We're like chequered chess pieces on a board
getting drawn into manoeuvres of greed and gluttony,
forever stuck on the stubbornness of our own profanity.

We need to stop fighting and just give in.
Acclimatise our minds to this idea of idealism
instead of imperialism
and stop chasing material things.

The pursuance of the superficial bling
that's bringing us into disrepute with our planet.
This universe has had enough of us,
increasing natural disasters are kicking our asses.

We need to turn it in,
before the universe starts turning in on us
to spontaneously combust and express its disgust at us.
Or maybe that's just the must we need.

Maybe we'll never be at ease.
Maybe we'll never experience true freedom
or ever see true peace.
At least not until, not until we've exhausted all the extremities,
all the natural resources, the God-given gifts
that replenish this existence we live in.
Not till the sun stops smiling,
the moon declines to give us light at night.

Not till every river has run dry
and the leaves of every tree have been scorched
in rainforest fires
by frustrated kids that live in high rises.

Not till every last tear drop erodes the mountain tops,
and we are swimming in our own sorrow,
watching the earth quake in its own grief.

Will we ever see
that you cannot eat money?

See one day we're going to wake up
in the aftermath of the wreckage of our past
to face the utmost certainty,
that this was all just forbidden fantasy,
that this was really just a game.

And all because we never sought to see things the same,
it was never going to change in the right places.

Hope is the drug every offender needs

JUDGEMENT ROOM

You don't really know me.
See you only really know what you hear, read,
and believe you see,
But what you know about me, don't define me.
So you don't really know me.

My past is not a reflection of my presence.
In essence I exist in spiritual consistency,
which has to be felt and not seen to be perceived properly.
So if you're looking at me,
through the perception of your eyes,
then you won't really see me.

All flesh just festers in illusion,
and perfection comes alive at the point of death.
That's not my experience,
that's just my fantasy,
my hope, my theory,
my guess for the best of the rest of life expectancy.
So if you really want to try me,
I say step
into my judgement room.

Welcome to my judgement room,
where there's barely room for two
but just leave your ego and your pride outside
and allow the commonality of your mind to slide in,
just glide in and gleefully spare some time
and take a seat for me.

Make yourself at home,
but be prepared to become as un-relaxed
and uncomfortable as possible
as we get philosophical
about what it really means to be a human being,
living with iniquity.

So, first, let me apologise
for my inadequacies, my insularity,
the informality of an invitation to this unfurnished property.
Cos, as you will see, there's no mirrors on the wall,
so you are bound to fall short of your own reflection.

So as a gesture to a guest,
I'll objectively give you the opportunity to start with me.
Or, better still, let me take the liberty
of illuminating every nook and cranny,
all the shit, the nitty-gritty that life's given me.

And if, at the end, empathy still defies you,
then you can throw your ten-pence worth in
as a tip for my hospitality.
And I say welcome
to this judgement room.

You can judge me by the pigmentation of my skin,
but that was God-given,
driven down from my ancestors into my next of kin,
and I didn't even get a look in.
So, I say, let's start again.
And I say welcome
to this judgement room.

You can judge me by my personality
but the reality is, none of us are infallible.
My morality is breakable and interchangeable
dependent upon my circumstances
and who I'm trying to impress.

Cos sometimes we dress up our best
but don't judge me by my clothes cos I didn't make them.
Whilst they might speak for my hygiene,
they're really just a front to cover me,
tailor made to suit my liabilities.

Cos I'm not brave enough to show you my balls,
my mouth's really big, but my courage is comparatively small.
We're all able and capable of wearing disguises,
so what I'm really trying to say is,
in the naked sense of this world,
vulnerability is not a designer label.

You can judge by my speech, my character, my swagger
and the way that I walk,
but more fool you cos even parrots can talk.
See I'll never tell you to walk a mile in my shoes,
I just say welcome
to this judgement room.

Welcome to my history, the struggle, the difficulty,
to find my rightful place in society.
Welcome to the fundamental injustice
that makes it nigh on impossible for a guy like me
to gain employability.
The convictions that have outcasted me,
this darkness that continues to blacken my serenity.

Welcome to the ignorance of those in a professional capacity.
All those voices of hierarchy that cry for change,
yet remain estranged to the concept.

And they say how and when will this great war be won?
And I say not until,
not until we begin to re-think the bill, the constitution,
this institution of trial and retribution.
Not until we begin to refine and redefine
the definition of desistance,
the long arm of the law that won't let go,
the rehabilitation of an offender that goes on forever,
the disclosure of a closed chapter
that imposes limitations on my future.

You keep on sticking this stigma on my ass.
This CRB mentality that keeps me prisoner to my past.
See I'm free from the jails but I can still see the bars.
Intelligence, surveillance, baby-sat in supervision,
forced onto courses to bring about an action of remorse
when it has to come from my own accord.

It's then multiplied and magnified
by the self-fulfilling prophecy
of the labels you bestow on me:
"Junkie, ex-offender, service user, thief."
I don't care how many text books you read,
or degrees you receive,
I'm fully qualified to tell you,
we are what we believe.
And we don't need academics to tell our story.

Thanks for your treatment programmes and your therapies
but what I really need is a chance to become
an acceptable, responsible,
productive member of my community;
a voice that can be heard,
a voice that can speak for its own self-worth.

The guilt, the shame, the remorse,
just made me feel worthless.
Surely my solution lies in re-evaluated self-esteem
and redirected purpose.

I'll grow when I'm ready, just help me plant the seed.
Because hope is the drug that every offender needs.
A new identity indentation, a source of inspiration.
So show me examples of the people that succeeded,
so I too can believe that I'm valued and needed.

Like a soldier with vigorous valour to confront this war,
my elders taught me that I had to find a cause
worth living and worth dying for.

Now I've found a calling that's connected to a cause,
a cause that uses metaphor to expose the flaws
in our criminal injustice system.

The internal revolution has risen and motivated and driven
to have my judgement reversed and my Karma forgiven;
to observe my blessed self-worth
and question why I've been preserved.

"Why why why?"
"Why didn't I die?"
It can only be to touch the hearts of those
that still feel doomed.
I'm out here trying to pay my dues.

And I say welcome
to your judgement room.

Hope means no-one is beyond redemption

HOPE

There's a song in our souls that sings for more
and it's chorus is full of hope.
It is the treatment of all spiritual sickness
but never the cure.
Hope

It is the road less travelled that has no destination,
cos no matter how far you've come on this journey
you cannot escape the inevitable need for
Hope

Regardless of our present situation
through the interchangeable fuses of our lives
we are defied at times by that one liner,
that illusive quotation.
The one that defines all universeral language,
the one that, without which, all other virtues would not exist.
It's constantly defended by faith and courage.
The one that typifies and signifies
the underlying message of all spiritual notes.
Hope

Let me break it down for you!
Hope
H-O-P-E
Happy Other People Exist

Hope
H-O-P-E
Harnessing Other People's Experiences
Positive and negative

Hope
H-O-P-E
Having Open Perception to Education
so you can learn from it.
Hope

If at any time you're struggling to remember
hope is
H-O-P-E
The Halo Over Promised Emancipation
regardless of the situation.

Keep on persevering,
you will see hope become a tangible reality.

You will feel hope
H-O-P-E
Hearty Old Processes Ended
HOPE HOPE HOPE

I'm gonna ram it down your throat
until you're sick of it.
Until it cuts your insides and starts to bleed your insecurities.
Until it seeps into your skin and starts to define you.
Till no boundaries can confine you.
Till the sky is never too high for you to soar through.

Its proper propaganda to believe
you should never have your head in the clouds
cos we were born to stand out
to get higher and higher
more clear and philosophical.

Hope is the antidote
to surpressing your perception of the possible.
Cos hope loves you, you, you,
you with all your warts and all your flaws
and all these rules and all these laws.

Cos God doesn't make mistakes
he just made us in a way
where you can learn from yours.
Cos hope means no-one's beyond redemption.

Everybody's got a dignity
that needs to be affirmed
with the correct attention.

Cos hope exists for this very reason
to weather the storms and the rainy seasons
so no matter how far down the scale you go
I want you to know
that this poem is with you.

Cos we've all got grace,
we've all got scope
if no matter what happens
we just be willing
to just keep clinging to
HOPE.

a beacon
of hope
and an
inspiration
to others

REFLECTIONS ON STEVE DUNCAN

Marilyn Harrison
Mentor

"Steven is a wizard with words, a beacon of hope and an inspiration to others, particularly those people who have been separated from society and not given the rite of passage to return.

"I have been privileged to have been given the role to support, mentor and encourage Steven to continue to share his stories through his spoken word poetry that manages to connect to people in such a unique and powerful way."

Colin Salmon,
Actor

"We stand alone together but I am shoulder to shoulder with Steve. Great work!"

Mary Ward-Lowery
Producer, BBC Poetry Please

"Steve is an alchemist with words. He puts his finger on the emotional truth of his subject and holds you spellbound."

Annette Hennessy
Chief Executive, Merseyside Community Rehabilitation

"Steve's words remind us of the power of the human spirit, why we do this work and what matters.

Whatever side of the tracks we are on there is more that binds us than we think. We all rise and fall with the challenges we face, we all need to feel that we belong, we all need to have hope for the future.

Steve came to Merseyside to help with our training but he helped us to so much more: to have confidence, to value what we do and to respect the people we work with. Read his words and think."

Sally Lewis
Chief Executive, Avon & Somerset Probation Trust (2013)

"Steve's talent arises from his innate feel for language and simply beautiful use of words. There is a pervading truth and optimism that shines through all of his work."

Communicating from the heart

for
Motivational Speaking | Performance Poetry
Desistance Workshops
www.insiderinsight.co.uk
info@insiderinsight.co.uk

glennie
communications group

for
Justice Communications
Publishing | Films | Websites
www.glennie.com
twitter @ianglennie